THE
WINDOW OF CERTAINTY

THE WINDOW OF CERTAINTY

Defining What Matters in Your School.

Exploring the Difference it Makes.

Rob Stones
Judy Hatswell

'The Window of Certainty'

A handbook for creating alignment in your school.
First published 2016.

Author: Rob Stones
Based on an original concept developed by Judy Hatswell

Editing and presentation advice: Valerie Stones

Copyright to this work is asserted by and jointly owned by:
Rob Stones of FutureShape Consulting
Judy Hatswell of Judy Hatswell and Associates.

Apart from any use permitted under the Copyright Act 1968, no portion of this book may be reproduced or printed without permission.
All rights reserved.

National Library of Australia
Cataloguing-in-publication data
Stones R
Hatswell J
The WINDOW of CERTAINTY
Defining What Matters in Your School, Discovering the Difference it Makes

ISBN 978-0-646-94930-7

1. EDUCATION / Leadership   2. EDUCATION / ADMINISTRATION

Rob Stones and Judy Hatswell are Instructors with the William Glasser Institute
www.wgia.org.au

For more information about the developers go to:
Rob's website: www.futureshape.com.au
Judy's website: www.judyhatswell.com

TABLE OF CONTENTS

Introduction 10

Chapter 1
Why a 'Window of Certainty'? 13

Chapter 2
What is the 'Window of Certainty'? 16
The four frames of the 'Window' 17

Chapter 3
Why a 'Window of Certainty' is Effective 21
Autonomy is energising 21
Internal Motivation and the 'Window' 22

CHAPTER 4
The 'Window of Certainty' is Need-Fulfilling 27
Survival and Certainty 28
Why People welcome Certainty and Purpose 29

Chapter 5
The 'Window of Certainty' is positive 32
The 'Window' harnesses the Power of Clear Direction 33

Chapter 6
The importance of the 'Values' and 'Beliefs' Frames 36
Shared Values promote the culture 37
Shared beliefs are productive 39

Chapter 7
Initiating 'Window of Certainty' Conversations 41
The 'Window' must be a co-creation 44

Chapter 8
How to Construct the 'Window of Certainty'   47
When to start   47

Which of the Frames comes first?   48
Creating Opportunity for the Conversations   50

Chapter 9
Constructing the Four Frames   53
Constructing the Vision Frame   53
Constructing the Outcomes Frame   57
Constructing the Values Frame   61
Constructing the Beliefs Frame   64

Chapter 10
What do you Risk without a 'Window of Certainty'?   68

Section 2
The 'Window of Certainty' Technical Manual   71
This section contains descriptions of detailed processes that might be used in creating a 'Window of Certainty'

Chapter 11
Creating the Vision   72

Chapter 12
Defining the Outcomes   80

Chapter 13
Agreeing the Values   86

Chapter 14
Choosing Useful Beliefs   97

Chapter 15
An example 'Window': Enterprise Road High School   107

Notes and References   112

INTRODUCTION

Watch an Olympic sprinter accelerating from the blocks. Every part is focused upon the goal. There is no extraneous movement to disturb balance. Effort is not wasted.

Listen to a great choir singing in harmony. There is no discord between the parts. Every note sung contributes to the rich and satisfying sound that they are creating together.

Feel your own sense of power and purpose in work and leisure when you are certain of where you are going and why it is important to you to achieve your goal.

There is a simplicity about these peak experiences that offers us a compelling metaphor for an organisation that wishes to be transparently focused, and in which the people who work and learn there are in in accord.

The 'Window of Certainty' is a guide for educational leaders who would like to build a culture of powerful alignment in their own complex organisation.

In your school, the 'Window of Certainty' will be a framework for gathering and expressing the unifying intentions and practices that will deepen the sense of alignment and shared purpose.

It will enable you to assemble your vision, desired outcomes, cultural values and constructive beliefs in one systematic representation, so that it easily becomes a reference point for the whole organisation.

Although I had often attempted to assemble similar frameworks in my own practice as a school leader, I first encountered what has come to be known as the 'Window of Certainty' in mid 2013. Judy Hatswell and I had just begun the first workshop in 'The Art of Leadership' - our initial collaboration as workshop facilitators. On that first morning, Judy informally sketched the four elements of a 'Window of Safety' as a way of framing common purpose in a school. She had been developing and sharing her intuitive understanding of the relationships between four powerful ideas for almost a decade.

After that workshop, several participants asked us to help them create the 'Window' in their own schools. Because I had previous experience of facilitating processes to develop each of the elements that made up the four frames of the 'Window', I hurriedly assembled a rather superficial elaboration of the 'Window of Safety' and sent it to the participants in our workshops.

Since that time, Judy and I have discussed and reflected upon the 'Window' many times, both between ourselves and also with the hundreds of school leaders with whom we have shared the concept and the processes that emerge from it.

The name the 'Window of Safety' has morphed to become the 'Window of Certainty'. We have subsequently elucidated the rationale of the 'Window' in more depth. At the request of many of these leaders, I have undertaken the task of composing this comprehensive guide to developing the 'Window' in a school community. This book not only describes in detail processes for developing a 'Window of Certainty', but also offers a thorough exploration of the theoretical perspectives that justify the time that this will take.

Judy and I have received extraordinary feedback about the usefulness of this approach to creating alignment, certainty and commitment in a school. This book has been written in order for us to share these powerful ideas with a wider audience.

Rob Stones,
November 2015

Defining What Matters In Your School

CHAPTER ONE

Why a 'Window of Certainty'?

The 'Window' is a framework that can provide a foundation for unity and alignment in your school. Built upon a set of defining conversations, it is a powerful way for leaders to initiate and develop the narrative that brings the school together. A 'Window of Certainty' provides a common understanding of what matters and why.

Schools often operate as a collection of independent professionals working behind closed doors; most of the teachers working hard, but each pursuing their own independent (and sometimes idiosyncratic) agenda. When schools operate like this, outcomes can vary widely within the school because there is too little alignment of purpose, strategy and teaching practice.

When leaders choose to develop the school as a collaboration of professionals, each learning from their colleagues and each in turn sharing their developing learning and expertise, the effectiveness of every teacher is progressively enhanced. It is this model of the school - as a collegial, interdependent organisation committed to the mutual improvement of the practice of teaching and learning - that is constructed using the 'Window of Certainty'.

The 'Window' is a pragmatic tool. It provides the answer to four significant questions that must be addressed by leaders who want to provide a clear direction as a basis for school effectiveness:

1. Where are we going? (Vision)
2. What will count as success? (Outcomes)
3. What should guide our practice? (Beliefs)
4. What is the culture that will drive our school's effectiveness? (Values)

These answers to these four critical questions provide the basis for the window that you will create.

The 'Window of Certainty' contains elements of paradox; it holds in tension the human desire for autonomy with the necessity for that freedom to have clear reference points and ultimate limits. Autonomy is motivating and energizing, but it must have boundaries if it is to coexist with collaboration and unity.

A defining feature of the 'Window of Certainty' approach is that is describes and encourages the personal freedom that will maximize creative engagement in the school, while also offering clear direction for cohesive effort and the alignment of actions.

Many schools develop processes for defining what is expected and allowed, but they often do this in a controlling way. Control does not liberate the energy that is generated when autonomous professionals are encouraged to exercise their freedoms. There may be certainty about direction and as to what is not permitted, but it comes at the cost of energised independence.

Other organizations encourage unfettered freedoms, but risk the distractions created when the exercise of personal flexibility is not accompanied by the responsibility to channel this individuality into the greater good of the school.

The 'Window of Certainty' provides balance. It is a framework that encourages personal autonomy while anchoring this independence to clear reference points: the vision, values and strategic orientation of the school as a whole.

In creating a framework for school effectiveness, both certainty and autonomy are required.

Certainty provides for clear direction; it unites collegial intentions and provides a clearly articulated culture of ethical action and professional behaviour.

Autonomy liberates individuals within the school to bring their own personal capabilities to the enterprise. This licence for them to exercise personal freedom taps into the wellspring of individual responsibility; it releases the energy that is created when individuals are driven by their own internal motivation, and pursue their work for its intrinsic rewards.

The main focus of this book is the creation of a 'Window of Certainty' for the whole school. However, teams within a school can (and do) create their own 'Windows'. It has also been encouraging to hear about classroom teachers who are using the 'Window of Certainty' as an alternative to 'classroom rules', thereby creating an enhanced sense of purpose and alignment within their own classrooms.

Exploring The Difference It Makes

CHAPTER TWO

What is the 'Window of Certainty'?

The 'Window of Certainty' includes the visioning and outcomes focus that are common in schools - but goes further.

The 'Window' consists of 4 Frames that define the zone within which the school community can work with freedom and creativity. The Frames provide direction for our autonomy, and also describe the limits of our independence.

In every school, leaders and teachers who are clear about these boundaries and directions are liberated to pour their energy into their work with confidence. The framework provides clear direction, but encourages creative professionalism. Teachers, whose work is often hidden from each other by the classroom walls, can experience a pervading sense of shared purpose by establishing common reference points for their endeavours.

The Frames of the 'Window of Certainty' provide these reference points and develop the shared purpose. They also provide clarity for the whole school community about what is expected and what is regarded as 'quality' in the work done in the school.

When leaders take the time and energy to create a 'Window of Certainty', their commitment sends a signal that highlights the importance of collaborative endeavour. The activity of defining the school's 'Window of Certainty' is itself a rich source of productive professional conversation. In more than one sense, the journey of reflection, and the collaborative discourse that is held upon the way, are as important as the product.

The 'Window of Certainty' has 4 Frames:

The Vision Frame

Exploring The Difference It Makes

Vision is an aspirational expression of intent; a realistic but imaginative dream; a stretch goal for the future. The realism is as important as the dreaming. Reaching for the 'just-beyond-our-present-grasp' is far more motivating than aiming for a distant possibility shrouded in vaguely aspirational statements.

Purpose is the pragmatic expression of vision. Purpose is more concrete and short-term; it describes the vision in specific terms that include the steps on the way. It charts the school's progress through its explicit and more immediate improvement agenda.

In each case they key question is: "Where are we going?"

The Outcomes Frame

Outcomes help to define the purpose in such a way that progress can be assessed. Outcomes can be short-term or long-term, describing either the results we will finally achieve when our vision becomes reality, or the interim outcomes through which we will measure our progress towards our long-term goals.

Without well-defined and measureable outcomes, vision can lack the clear-cut direction required. When the outcomes associated with the vision are elucidated, the organisation can measure its march towards success.

The questions for outcomes are:

"What will success look like?"

"How will we measure our progress?"

The Values Frame – 'Values in Action'

Values, in this context, are the critical foundation of culture: 'This is the way we do things around here'.

There is a distinction between these values-in-action and theoretical 'principles'. For example, many people will intuitively agree that they value 'respect', but without discussion and consensus this value is enacted in many different ways in the school. The focus of the Values Frame is not simply to identify ethical principles that members of the school community hold in common, but to spell out what these mean in practice.

Exploring The Difference It Makes

The question for the Values Frame is: "What values should underpin the way we work and interact with each other?"

The Beliefs Frame

Beliefs are our ideas about how things work. They guide our strategies because they are our trusted perceptions of the world - what we accept as 'true in our experience'. As individuals, our different repertoires of experience lead to very different intuitive assumptions about effective practice. Consequently, this frame of the 'Window' is often the longest conversation, and the most likely to be ongoing.

When embedded in the context of collegial conversation the questions that can be most helpful are:
"What beliefs guide the most effective practice?" or
"What beliefs will be most useful in achieving our vision?"

CHAPTER THREE

Why a 'Window of Certainty' is Effective.

The 'Window' is an effective tool for creating alignment because the four elements of the 'Window' are the critical dimensions of unified thinking in a school. The teachers and leaders who work together to create exceptional outcomes need to be sure about what they are aiming for, and why it matters; what will work to achieve the goal; and how they should behave to maintain the cohesion of their work together.

The 'Window' brings about engagement through encouraging autonomy, but harnesses that autonomy by defining the boundaries within which freedom is exercised.

Autonomy is energising!

The author and researcher Edward Deci[1] suggests that autonomy is the key to responsible self-regulation. Deci's research and conclusions point to a clear message: when we harness each individual's autonomy, he or she is likely to be more, not less, responsible. Freed to be the authors of their own behaviours, people are more willing to focus on their own mastery of practice and tend to embrace their activities with a sense of self-interest and commitment.

Deci's research also reveals, time and again, that when individuals feel 'controlled', they are at best compliant and at worse resistant: *"Push me and I will tend to push back!"*

Exploring The Difference It Makes

The more we try to control the behaviours of our teachers and our students by hedging them around with the mechanisms of control (rules, rigidity and authoritarianism), the more they are likely to become disengaged and antagonistic.
Similarly, Dr. William Glasser[2], a pioneer of the psychology of internal control, powerfully argued his belief that:
"Freedom may be the defining human characteristic; it is our ability to be constructively creative." Glasser believed that striving to be autonomous: to be able to do things our own way; the author of our own success and failure, are built into our genetic imprinting.

At the heart of this emphasis on autonomy is my belief, shared with Deci and Glasser, that people are self-determined and internally motivated. Striving for personal autonomy is a critical element of this internal motivation, and is the reason that the 'Window of Certainty' is so powerful.

Internal Motivation and the 'Window'.

The key to success in school leadership is the ability to influence the staff to work together to achieve the goals of the school.

Influence, persuasion, communicating with staff in such a way that you can secure a commitment from them in the interests of the school, are central to leadership. For that reason, a profound understanding of human behaviour and motivation is vital. When school leaders understand the working of the human mind, they are able to tune their own behaviour in order to be ethically influential.

Defining What Matters In Your School

A disturbingly common belief (embedded in the language of ordinary discourse) is that motivation comes from outside us: other people or events are responsible for our actions, our mistakes and our unhappiness. This external control paradigm is damaging to relationships, and in the world of work produces the coercive and manipulative strategies that people in authority tend to use to get their own way. It also generates the resistance and shirking of responsibility that are common in people who are being 'controlled'. As Deci[3] writes: "External pressure can sometimes bring about compliance, but with compliance come various negative consequences, including the urge to defy."

Knowing that behaviour is a composite of four elements is a good starting point for understanding human behaviour. Behaviour is more than just action; it also includes the thinking, emotions and physiology that are indivisible from the action itself. All behaviour is an aggregate of these four components. Just as the car has four wheels, people have four interrelated functions that make up their conduct.

Because all behaviour always includes these four functions, influential leaders respect and connect with the thinking and feeling of the people they work with, not just their actions. The 'Window of Certainty' must be created using processes that recognise the connections between thinking, feeling and personal engagement.

23

Exploring The Difference It Makes

A great misconception about leadership is that position-power is all that is needed to be influential. The reality is that there are elements of power that are potentially disconnecting and which actually create resistance. The assumption that all a leader needs to do is to 'tell people what they should do' is naïve, but prevalent. The idea that leaders not only have the right to issue instructions, but that people do and should respond by doing as they are told, is a prevailing myth that disregards what we know about the brain.

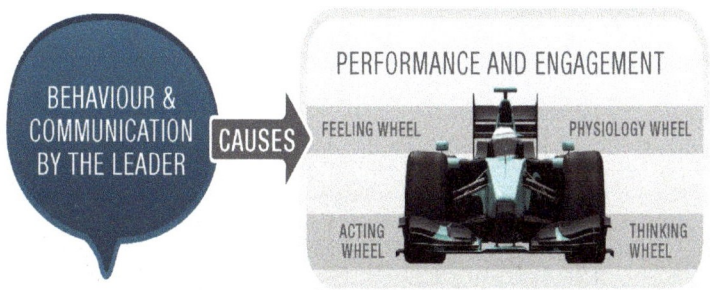

Teachers and students are not 'passive responders' as implied by the diagram above. All individuals are actively engaged with the people and events around them. Inside the 'invisible' mind of each person are the processes of awareness, interpretation and judgment (choice) that create their unique response to the actions of others and to the events occurring in their world.

From outside the individual, this hidden process seems like a 'black box': we can't know exactly how any other person is seeing things, making sense of them and deciding what to do. What we observe is the end result.

Defining What Matters In Your School

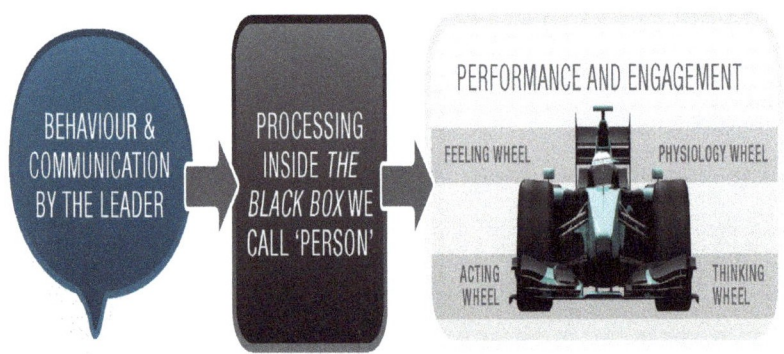

However, from our own internal experience as well as from the research of reputable psychologists and neuroscientists, we do know a great deal about what is in the 'black box' we call a person. As leaders, we can use that knowledge to support the creation of a 'Window of Certainty' in our school: a 'Window' that will support the full engagement and commitment of our teachers.

Within each person are the schemas, accumulated throughout life. From the moment of birth, each human organism interacts with the stimuli that are filtered through his or her sensory system to create patterns of neural connections that we call schemas. The schemas we have already created help us interpret the new information we are receiving through our senses, and then process the resulting information to generate new or more elaborate schemas – which in turn becomes the revised basis for our unique perceptions of the world.

The thinking created by this neurological activity rises to the level of consciousness when we pay attention; when we concentrate hard on a task; when we listen or observe

Exploring The Difference It Makes

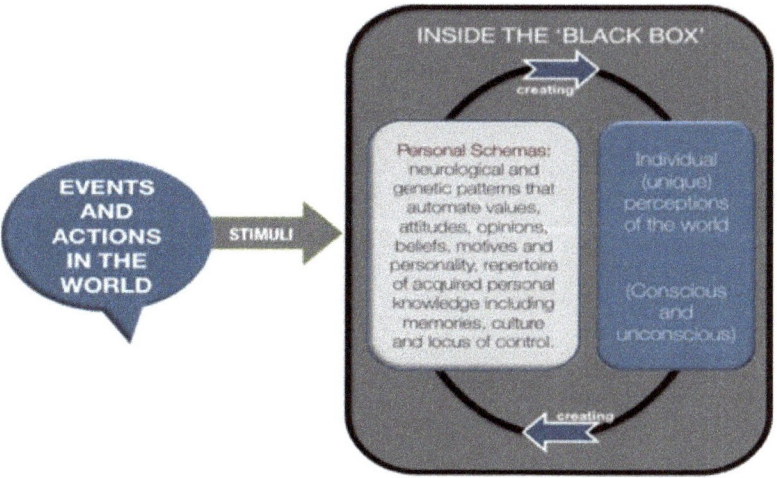

something carefully. However, a great deal of the 'thought' associated with our neurological activity is not conscious, instead it is 'automated'. That's necessary. Our brain would be paralysed if we had to consciously process each new sensory input. Instead, we leave our nervous system to go about its business behind the scenes: filtering out sensory data, comparing new information to old in order to make sense of it, and storing the result for a time when we will need to summon it to consciousness.

There are two features of this ongoing operation that are the key to connecting with and influencing other people.

The first is that we are all genetically programmed to meet our individual needs. The second is that, however socialised we are, we all retain some of the instinctive behaviour of our primitive forbears. Each of these features operates powerfully in the workplace, and leaders who understand them are well positioned to create the context in which their staff and students will collaborate to produce their best work.

CHAPTER FOUR

The 'Window of Certainty' is Need-Fulfilling.

Every person, every teacher and student, is intrinsically motivated to serve his or her own genetic needs. Although different researchers and writers identify these needs using slightly different words, there is a huge amount of common ground[4]:
- We all have a need for achievement: power; status; control of our lives; increasing responsibility.
- We all seek autonomy: to be the authors of our own lives; to be self–determining; to be creative.
- Need-satisfying relationships are essential for everyone: relationships in which we will find love; friendship; acceptance; feelings of connection.
- Every individual is driven to learn, and to get pleasure from that learning.
- We also seek meaning in our lives: the sense that what we are engaged in is important and consequential.

It is these genetic needs that direct the orientation of our schemas. Every time we experience something as need-satisfying, we store the memory of it and actively seek to reproduce that experience – and the chemical reward that goes with the experience. When something feels good or feels right, it's because our brain has just released some dopamine (or one of the body's other pleasure-inducing chemicals) into our system.

It is energising to work in a school where we have autonomy; where we can achieve; where we relate well to those around us; where we learn constantly and believe there is meaning and purpose in our professional lives. Working in a school like this feels great! It's that environment which the 'Window of Certainty' is intended to create.

Survival and Certainty.

The need that I omitted from the list above is the need for survival. The survival need is very important to our understanding of the 'Window of Certainty', but it operates in quite a different way from the other needs.

The need for survival is deeply embedded in the reptilian remnant that still lurks at the base of our evolved brain. It works with the emotional brain to keep us constantly alert for danger. This primitive brain function is designed to respond far more quickly than our slower rational cognition. When survival is at stake, there is no time to lose!

Complicating the way that the need for survival affects our behaviour is the social environment in which we are embedded. 'Social survival' is now as much a feature of our primitive reactions as physical survival. It also has a chemical basis. Our emotional brain gears us for avoidance or aggression whenever a threat is perceived, by injecting adrenalin or norepinephrine into our metabolism: this is useful for aggression or resistance, but not helpful for trust and harmony!

The result is that if actions or events around us are perceived as potentially threatening, they trigger defensive activity through the emotional brain. Neuroscience writer

David Rock[5] explains that we react emotionally when we perceive threats through:
- An apparent negative change to our status;
- A sense that something is unfair;
- Uncertainty about the purpose of our activity or what's expected of us;
- Uncomfortable relationships: when we don't trust or relate to those with whom we work;
- Limits to our autonomy: not having the freedom to do things in our own way or to put our personal stamp on our work.

Rock[5] describes how these apparent threats trigger the brain's emotional thinking pathways, and 'flight' or 'fight' mechanisms are automatically activated. In his paper on brain-based threats to personal influence, Rock[5] writes: "A reduction in autonomy, for example when being micro-managed, can generate a strong threat response."

Writing about procedures within organisations, Rock[5] suggests that: "Sound policy establishes the boundaries within which individuals can exercise their creativity and autonomy. In this regard, sound policy hard-wires autonomy into the processes of an organisation." It is this kind of hard-wiring that the 'Window of Certainty' offers.

Why People Welcome Certainty and Purpose.

Almost everyone likes to be confident about their place in the world and the purpose of the institutions in which they work. Doubt and confusion are experienced as an undercurrent of threat, to which certainty and a sense of shared purpose are the antidotes. In an environment where teachers are sure of the school's direction and are confident about what is expected of them, a sense of safety emerges, and everyone is open to working collegially.

Certainty, as we have seen, is embedded in all of the human needs. It is not only the social expression of the human need for survival, it also provides for structures that define productive relationships. Certainty gives direction to the need for power and achievement. Critically, within an educational institution, a reasonable level of certainty provides a foundation for the processes and practices that lead to effective learning.

A sense of certainty also provides a balance to the exercise of autonomy. While autonomy supports individual achievement, certainty helps create unity and rewarding professional relationships. The two dynamics - autonomy and boundaries - are not mutually exclusive. The research of Ryan and Koestner[6] discovered that when limits are set in an autonomy-supportive manner, they not only support creativity, but also encourage responsibility and intrinsic motivation.

While freedom without common direction has the potential to undermine collaborative effort and team alignment, certainty about the school's direction and purpose is the glue that binds the efforts of autonomous individuals to the common intention of the enterprise.

As our needs for certainty and autonomy influence each other, we usually feel more confident to exercise our freedoms when the expectations and the boundaries are clear; when we know what is expected and approved and what is not. Knowing the parameters of our independence is somehow more liberating than absolute freedom.

Barnes Boffey[7] uses an allegory about horses set free in a paddock: "When the enclosure is tiny, the horses are fractious and grumpy with each other: too little autonomy is irritating and limiting. When the paddock is huge, the horses run wild, confused and unruly in the absence of visible limits. However, when the boundaries are clear, but provide room to move, the horses co-exist contentedly."

Like Boffey's horses, we are relational creatures. Our status among our peers; our relationships with them; our sense that the world should be fair; our need to have meaningful direction in our working life, are all self-imposed limits to our desire for autonomy.

If we are uncertain about the parameters of our work, we are hindered from applying our creativity to students' learning by the little voice of doubt that warns us that this may not be acceptable. While it feels great to be working at the 'frontiers' of professional practice, we can feel very exposed if this is accompanied by a sense of uncertainty. Fear does not help us to be at our creative best!

The 'Window of Certainty' offers optimal independence within clear limits. The Frames provide the boundaries that our need for certainty requires. Within these limits, our entrepreneurial spirit can operate with validation. This framework encourages us to use our imaginative autonomy to create rich learning experiences and powerful collaborations.

Exploring The Difference It Makes

CHAPTER FIVE

The 'Window of Certainty' is Positive!

When you think about the 'Window of Certainty' for your school, the focus must be on what you want rather than what you don't want; what is inside the frames, not what is outside them. This is a positive framing of what you expect and encourage.

The idea of establishing a framework of clear direction for the work people do in organizations is not new. But so often, what identifies these frames is what they exclude, rather than what they include. This typical "rules" approach generates a focus on what not to do rather than on what is encouraged.

In contrast to the rules perspective, this framework describes what is desirable, not what is frowned upon! The 'Window of Certainty' is based upon positive psychology – the psychology of the mental processes that lead to optimal performance. People do their best work when they are certain about what they are encouraged to do, and why this is valued. They are more inclined to be hesitant when they are anxious about straying into 'unacceptable' areas.

The traditional ways to describe the boundaries of behaviour through rules and laws tend to emphasise what is proscribed, with its attendant negativity. When individuals cross the boundaries, there are real or implied consequences. Not only is this an ineffective way to engage and enthuse staff in positive actions, it also creates the potential for resistance.

The 'Window' is a symbol of positive empowerment. It describes the deliberate design of the ideas, behaviours and strategies that the school believes will lead to success. It guides you towards where you want your school to go and how you want your people to behave.

The 4 Frames are drawn inside the 'Window' to emphasise that this is what the school **wants,** rather than what it excludes.

'The Window' harnesses the Power of Clear Direction.

The 'Window of Certainty' does more than provide boundaries for the autonomy of individuals. By offering clear direction, it also reduces the likelihood of energy-sapping distraction.

Exploring The Difference It Makes

The *FutureShape*[8] formula for effective performance is a simple one:

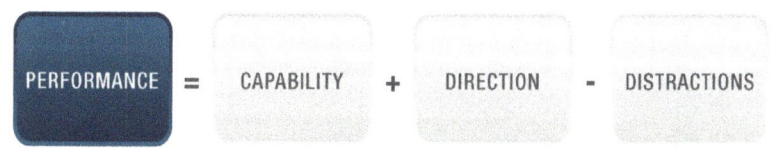

However capable we are as teachers and leaders, however supportive our parent community and enthusiastic our students; clear direction is required for effective performance. We need to know where we are going!

However, as most school leaders know only too well, the effective performance of a school is often undermined by distractions. Priorities that are suddenly imposed from other layers of governance; the uninformed expectations of the community; internal disputes and misunderstanding; all these sap the school's energy and draw attention from effective teaching and learning. Having a clearly articulated and well-understood 'Window of Certainty' is an effective instrument for resolving these distractions.

The substance of the 'Window' provides clear criteria on which the claims of external distractions are assessed. When they are not aligned with, or likely to contribute to, the vision and outcomes described in the 'Window of Certainty', they provide a reason for limiting the time and energy allocated to them. Unless the 'good idea' or 'recommended practice' will help the school achieve its vision, it will hurt it. This is a good reason for saying "No", or more tactfully, "Not right now"!

Defining What Matters In Your School

If the distractions are internal, the 'Window' provides the reference point to which staff and leaders can turn when disputes over practice or individual behaviours occur. The 'Window' also provides a vehicle for the resolution of conflict or the positive re-direction of energy when things do go awry.

The Frames of the 'Window' provide the touchstone to which members of the school community can constantly refer when the bustle of the daily life of the school narrows focus and confuses with distractions.

The 'Window of Certainty' is the 'big picture' to which everyone can turn when there is a need to remind themselves what really matters.

Exploring The Difference It Makes

CHAPTER SIX

The 'Values' and 'Beliefs' Frames.

These two frames make an important contribution to the 'Window of Certainty'.

The Values Frame helps to create the culture in which teacher and student engagement can underpin the school's success formula. **The Beliefs Frame** ensures that there is an emphasis on effective practice.

The Window contributes to a 'Culture of Effectiveness'.

The school culture is the pond in which all its fish swim.

When the pond is murky and confused, it's hard for individuals to perform well or come together as a team.

Culture also has profoundly ethical dimensions. When the culture is underpinned by positive values and uplifting beliefs, the morale of the professionals and students is enhanced.

Victor Frankl[9] identified the search for meaning as an important dimension of human resilience and inspiration. Energy is released and motivation is assured when teachers believe their work is meaningful, honourable and important.

Defining What Matters In Your School

The noble purpose of our profession connects a sense of deep meaning with the enterprise of teaching. This is one of the reasons why the Values and Beliefs Frames are important dimensions of the 'Window'.

Shared Values promote the culture.

Values provide guidance about how we will go about our business in the school; how we will create the culture in which our strategies will thrive. This Frame describes how we aspire to deal with other people (of all ages). It creates the ethical imperatives that can guide daily behaviours and relationships.

However inspiring the vision and attainable the outcomes, it is the embedded culture that most often makes a difference to the organisation. When Peter Drucker[10] said: "Culture eats strategy for breakfast," he was referring to the necessary pre-conditions of effective action. When culture is supportive and positive, much can be achieved that would be inhibited in a negative or ambivalent culture.

A common oversight of school leaders is to develop strategies that have the potential to produce the outcomes that the school's vision aspires to, without considering the culture that is needed for these strategies to be effective. Without a purposeful, enabling culture, potentially sound strategies are often lost in the distractions created by interpersonal confusion and conflict. *Many plants wither in poor soil!*

The identifying features of culture are the enacted values of the community - values that are embedded in behaviours. Many years ago, Chris Argyris[11] drew attention to the contradictions that manifest themselves in unreflective organisations. His research showed that the principles that people believed were fundamental to their plans, actions and explanations were often not consistent with the values that were revealed in their behaviours.

Argyris and Schon[11] assert that people hold maps in their heads about how to plan, implement and review their actions. They further explain that: **"Few people are aware that the maps they use to take action are not the theories they explicitly espouse**. Also, even fewer people are aware of the maps or theories they **do** use" (Argyris, 1980).

Argyris draws our attention to the truth that unless people are prepared to rigorously develop a culture of openness, participation and personal responsibility, the tendency for individuals to be defensive, self-referencing and controlling will emerge, and dominate their actual behaviour. This tacit culture will then undermine the school's declared aspirations.

If a community wants to ground its actions and intentions in a set of common values, then not only do those values have to be debated and agreed, but the behavioural implications of the agreed values must be clear. Only in that way can individuals be accountable to themselves (and to each other) for the standards they have agreed.

This means that the creation of an open, ethical and responsible culture, in which individuals are valued and support each other in their common purpose, must be deliberate. It will rarely happen accidentally. While the collaborative creation of the Values Frame of the 'Window of Certainty' is not all that must be done to generate an effective school culture, it is an essential beginning.

Shared Beliefs are productive.

The Beliefs Frame is similarly values-oriented, but beliefs go beyond values.

Beliefs are the trusted perceptions of the way the world works. In the context of education, they refer specifically to what works for effective learning to occur. A belief that learning progress is possible for all students, and that effective teaching practice can extend the capabilities of all students, would be a pre-requisite belief for teachers if the school were to be effective.
Without that underpinning belief, many strategies associated with differentiated learning or student-centered practice would be unconsciously sabotaged by the scepticism of the teachers. If a teacher has a model of the world in which some students are fundamentally incapable, why would he or she put energy into a practice that they are sure will fail?

Part of the difficulty is that, without reflection, people often tend to treat beliefs as if they were truths. As Robert Burton[12] points out, beliefs do **feel** like truths. In fact, as Burton explains, they are often simply our untested assumptions about how things work, based often on small parts of our experience.

Dr. Albert Mamary[13] used to draw the distinction between 'useful beliefs' and 'limiting beliefs'. As he would often exhort his teachers and other audiences: "Why choose limiting beliefs? Choose useful beliefs."

We can, in fact, adjust our perceptions of how the world works. We have many beliefs as children that become out-of-date as we grow up. Even as adults, beliefs that served a

Exploring The Difference It Makes

purpose at a particular time of out life can change when our knowledge expands or we move in a different context.

Beliefs are challenged by new information, reliable research and the success of effective practitioners who start from different assumptions. The Beliefs Frame of the 'Window' is where the school can explore the unproductive beliefs that are hindering effective practice, and thus look for more useful alternatives.

The sensitivity of this collaboration makes this the most complex frame to develop, but possibly the most important. When teachers adopt helpful beliefs that facilitate the adoption of effective practice, much of the self-doubt and uncertainty that hinder their best teaching are dissipated or reduced.

CHAPTER SEVEN

Initiating 'Window of Certainty' Conversations

The conversations required to establish a 'Window of Certainty' go deep - and they take time. Leaders sometimes hesitate to initiate these conversations because they fear the time they will take, and the divisions they might reveal.

When people talk about their values and beliefs, and they are asked to reflect on their common purpose, the conversations are often intense. However, although these discussions may seem to risk division because they tap into potential differences, they are eventually both insightful and healing.

To create alignment, cohesion and harmony, differences must be openly addressed and discussed. Wise leaders invest in these conversations, knowing that without deep understanding about why we are doing this work together in this way, alignment is not possible.

The very depth of the conversation may cause some initial perception of the deepening of difference. However, as Marco Korn[14] implies, unstated differences are more damaging to relationships and collaboration than those that are stated, explored, understood and resolved.

Exploring The Difference It Makes

'Window of Certainty' conversations do take time; but they conserve energy.

If this seems contradictory, then this image may help:

The ultimate aim of the 'Window of Certainty' is the creation of alignment in the school. We are aligned as an organisation when as close as possible to 100% of the energy is directed towards common outcomes. This is the condition for optimal performance.

Tolerating a situation where energy is wasted in misunderstanding, distraction, interpersonal conflict and erratic pedagogy may 'save time', but it dissipates energy.

Of all the frustrations we encounter as leaders, the sense that our school is being distracted by other agendas and competing priorities is the most debilitating. Remember the effectiveness formula:

Defining What Matters In Your School

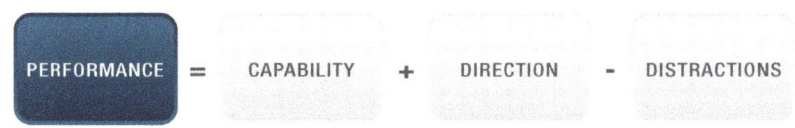

Time spent building capability, agreeing on common direction, exploring values and beliefs, and **removing distraction** is always a worthwhile investment.

Addressing the Questions Implicit in the 'Window'

The 'Window' answers the questions:
What are we about?
    Where we are going?
        How will we know if we are improving?
            What's the best way to do things?
            What matters?

And often the most important questions:
Why are we doing things this way?
    Why are relationships so important?

The purpose or vision of a school is often a published artifact, but very often it is not de-constructed in a way that spells out its significance for the work of teachers and students. As a result, it is common to find that a school's governing variables are obscure. Yet everything that we know about the unique nature of individual perception reminds us that taking for granted that there is a common understanding is at best optimistic, and at worst reckless. If the vision matters, it has to be clear to everyone what it is and why it matters.

Exploring The Difference It Makes

As my friend Richard is accustomed to say: "People with private visions may flourish in contemplative life, but they rarely contribute much to school leadership."

Without the common reference point provided by the 'Window of Certainty', hesitation about the right thing to do, or how things should be, is often complicated by the use of authority.

When issues of rectitude or principle depend for their resolution on the judgement of an authority figure (rather than any predetermined standard), we put 'the right thing to do' inside a file marked 'secret' that is often only opened after the event. The obscurity of this approach to what is right sets up a pointless guessing game for teachers, and a situation in which leaders can easily find themselves at odds with their staff because there is no agreed standard or expectation in place to which either can refer. The trust between leaders and their staff members can be the first casualty when only the leaders know what is 'right'.

With the 'Window of Certainty' in place, leaders can point to the agreements made in the 'Window' and say with clarity and confidence:
"**This** is the way we do things here, and **this** is why."

The 'Window of Certainty' must be a co-creation

Although the impetus for creating the 'Window' is usually the commitment of the leader, to be effective the 'Window' must become a co-creation.

The instrument for creating the 'Window of Certainty' is conversation. Making time for these conversations, and shaping them so that they are productive and move towards consensus, is a requisite leadership skill. The suggestions offered later in this publication, address some ways in which these discussions might be generated and shaped, as well as some ideas about how to prioritise the conversations in the busy life of the school.

For example, a 'Window of Certainty' might be created or visited when the school is about to embark on: a change process; a review and enhancement of assessment practices; the introduction of new structures or development related to the use of data for learning improvement; or a new program of professional review. A common use of the 'Window of Certainty' is the renewal or realignment of the leadership team, or any team in the school that has just acquired new membership or a new leader.

All of these could become the rationale for the creation of a new 'Window', or a review of an existing 'Window'.

The 'Window' is not only for the whole school

As mentioned earlier, this guide was created with a focus on the creation of a 'Window of Certainty' for the whole school. For that reason, the suggestions in the 'Technical Manual' about how to create a 'Window' assume that significant numbers of people will be involved, and that the activity of creating the 'Window' will require complex collaborative processes.

However, ever since Judy and I have been talking to teachers and schools about the 'Window', principals of very small schools, class teachers, team leaders, executive

Exploring The Difference It Makes

teams and working parties within schools have used the model to create alignment in their own unit.

The 'Window of Certainty' is an instrument for creating alignment wherever it is needed. It can be applied whenever there is a group or enterprise that wants to work with unity and cohesion. When a group is relatively small, the processes for creating the 'Window' will be far simpler than those that I have described for a large and complex institution.

However, almost all of the collaborative processes suggested in the 'Technical Manual' can be easily adapted for groups of a smaller size. Gathering the ideas of group members, and developing cohesion between them, usually becomes far simpler when the group is small.

CHAPTER EIGHT

How to Construct the 'Window of Certainty'

This guide is intended to be of assistance to anyone wishing to construct the Window of Certainty' in their own school, whatever the size of the school.

To this end, the 'Technical Manual' describes eleven collaborative processes, which can be used in large schools with complex settings. Smaller schools (or groups within a school) will be able to adapt and simplify these processes.

When to start?
The short answer is - as soon as possible! As soon as the 'Window of Certainty' is in place, everyone can refer to it when direction is needed. Leaders can point to the values, beliefs and outcomes specified by the 'Window' as a basis for 'Courageous Conversations'.

An ideal time to begin creating the 'Window of Certainty' is the point at which a leader takes up his or her position of school leadership, whether of the whole school or of a team within the school. However, that opportunity does not always present itself.

The reality is that school leaders can begin to create, or re-create, the 'Window of Certainty' when the need arises. Whenever that need occurs, there is a clear purpose for creating the certainty, describing the relatedness and defining the freedoms within which the staff of the school can work with energy and commitment.

It is important not to rush the creation of the 'Window of Certainty'. The power of the 'Window' is in the conversations that mark the journey of its creation, rather than the artefact. Ultimately, it is not the 'product' of a completed 'Window' that is transformational, but the conversations that take place during its creation.

Which of the 'Window Frames' comes first?

Because the four Frames of the 'Window' are different views of the future that is being created, there is no one place to start.

However, the vision for improvement or explicit improvement agenda identified by the leader (for or with the school community) is often the de-facto starting point.

There are times when burning issues that need to be resolved to unite the school swirl around values and relationships. At other times, explicit conversations with regard to beliefs (e.g. about which pedagogies or which ways of creating change are most likely to succeed) provide the impetus for the healing of divisive opinions.
In **most** situations, leaders begin with the vision and related outcomes, and then use these as a starting point to identifying the values that the vision embodies, and the beliefs that must underpin that vision. On other occasions, the school may be quite clear about the outcomes they want to achieve, and choose to map the other Frames from these outcomes.

The important thing is to keep in mind the ways in which the Frames are interactive.
So for example:

Defining What Matters In Your School

or, viewing the interactions of the Frames in the clockwise direction:

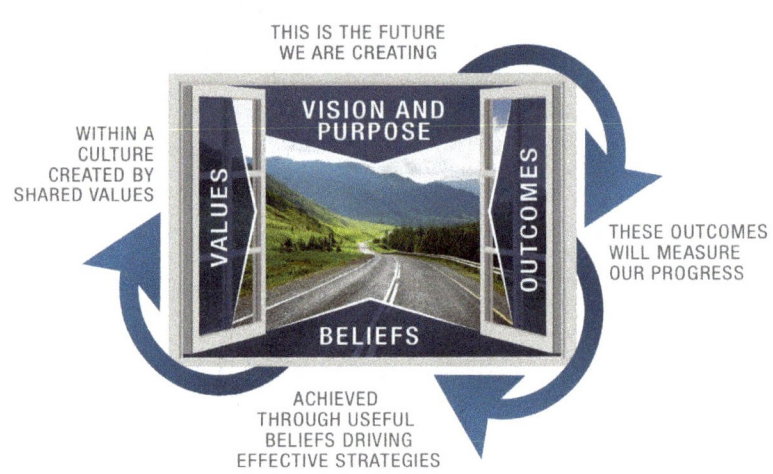

Constructed with the interplay between Frames firmly in mind, the 'Window of Certainty' will create and support the alignment of purpose and action.

Whatever starting point is chosen, the dialogues that create the 'Window of Certainty' overlap. The processes for creating the Frames are often similar, whatever the order in which they are addressed. For the purpose of this guide, each of the Frames is tackled separately. In practice, the parallel conversations that are generated through the consideration of any one Frame may mean that all four Frames are addressed and come together through one extended conversation.

Creating Opportunity for the Conversations

Because principals and teachers often perceive that they are 'time-poor', the deliberate creation of opportunities for 'Window of Certainty' conversations is important.

In actuality, there are many meetings and conversations in the school that are used for less important (though not always less urgent) matters. The possibilities are then either:
1. Use existing opportunities for 'Window of Certainty' dialogue.
2. Create additional opportunities for conversation about the 'Window of Certainty'.

1.
Use **existing meetings** for 'Window of Certainty' conversations:
- Leadership team meetings.
- Stage meetings.

- o   Faculty meetings.
- o   Sub-committee meetings.
- o   Full staff meetings.
- o   Professional Development days.
- o   P&C meetings.
- o   Class discussions.
- o   Classroom 'communities of inquiry'.
- o   Other small group meetings and discussions.

Formal meetings, even when they are not solely focused on the Frames of the 'Window of Certainty', can include cameos that can be found in the suggestions provided by this guide.

2.
Create meetings for 'Window of Certainty' Conversations:

- o Student-free days.
- o Breakfast Discussions.
- o Staff dinners.
- o Occasional collegial get-togethers.
- o Retreats for the leadership group or sections of the staff.
- o Major staff planning or renewal days.
- o Reframe review and development meetings as (at least partly) 'Window of Certainty' conversations.

In all these settings, the relationship-building nature of 'Window of Certainty' discussions adds an additional positive dimension to the conversation.

Making Time for the 'Meetings of Minds' is Essential

One consideration must be emphasised here. It seems to be increasingly common for schools to have very few 'meetings' other than those concerned with operational and managerial matters. Information is distributed electronically or in 'briefings', where one-way communication is the norm.

The author of this guide believes that substantive conversations are essential for both optimal performance and mental and emotional well-being.

These slower-paced, reflective conversations are the opportunities for teachers to learn collaboratively, broaden and deepen their professional understanding and build trust.

For the leaders, creating and participating in (not always leading) these conversations is demonstrably one of the most potent tools to increase their influence, both with the teachers they lead and on the outcomes for students[15].

When substantive conversations such as these are embedded in the workplace discourse of the school, finding opportunities for 'Window of Certainty' conversations will be straightforward. Where a school has developed the habit of faster, but more shallow, communication processes, constructing the 'Window of Certainty' will provide an opportunity to re-discover the power of deep professional discourse.

CHAPTER NINE

Constructing the Four Frames

Constructing The Vision Frame

Vision is the primary source of direction for the school: it is the process of 'thinking ahead' to the future that the school will inhabit when the improvement agenda has been embraced and the dream achieved.

Although vision should be aspirational, it must adopt the discipline of 'realistic optimism': that robust quality that leads us to bite off what we can chew - but only just! If the vision is seen as unattainable, it will not attract the energy of the staff. If it is seen as simply a minimal extension of 'business as usual', it will fail to inspire. Bringing an attractive vision into existence requires that a leader understands the school community well enough to know what will excite - and what will deter. According to Kouzes and Posner[16]:

"Being forward-looking - envisioning exciting possibilities and enlisting others in a shared view of the future - is the attribute that most distinguishes leaders from non – leaders."

If vision is the description of the desired future towards which the school will work, more immediate statements of Purpose often buttress the realisation of the vision. These statements of purpose chart the explicit improvement agenda that delineates the school's journey to the fulfilment of its plans. They form 'the stairway that brings hope to the dream'.

Creating the Vision

Although creating the vision is usually seen as the principal's primary responsibility, it is important that it is not his or hers alone. The process for creating the vision is not a sales pitch! It requires genuine harnessing of the optimism of the school community to the leader's own prescience and hopes.

Although most schools come to embrace elements of the vision of their leader, no leader can impose his or her vision upon others. As counterintuitive as it might seem: "The best way to lead people into the future is to connect with them deeply in the present. The only visions that take hold are shared visions." [16]

The creation of a powerful uniting vision requires that the Principal lead a thoughtfully guided process of collaboration. If the process is unguided or not well focused, the consensus that emerges is too often an adoption of the lowest common features of the community's thinking. This may recognise some sameness in the 'here and now', but won't lead into the future. The leader's job is to help the community spiral upwards into its most noble thinking and highest aspirations.

If the leader does not insist upon clarity and specificity, then what emerges is often a flabby motherhood statement – the most debilitating of all goal statements because it captures wishes, not wants. Motherhood statements are usually framed with such generality that failure is impossible – but so is success. Such limp statements of warm intention may briefly fire the emotions through a sense of recognition of good things, but provide no real direction or sustained enthusiasm.

An effective vision must be so specific that progress towards it can be measured; but also so consequential that it will inspire energy and enthusiasm.

To paraphrase Ruth Wageman's[17] description of a compelling purpose, a powerful vision must be:
- Clear enough to provide direction.
- Matter enough to energise everyone.
- Challenging enough to inspire, but still attainable.

If the above are guiding principles, the following are three visioning processes. Each process is collaborative in nature, although the degree of involvement varies with each one.

In the 'Technical Manual' three alternative visioning processes suggested are:

1. 'Fully collaborative.'
2. 'Editing the draft.'
3. 'Walking the leader's vision journey.'

Constructing The Outcomes Frame

Outcomes have three functions:
o To identify concrete and measurable products that will clarify elements of the vision.
o To help narrow and focus the school's purpose and improvement agenda.
o To provide feedback on the effectiveness of the school's journey towards its goals.

Useful outcomes are always verifiable. If an outcome statement is too general to be tested, or has so long a timeline that the relationship to the activity of the school seems tenuous, then it fails the test of usefulness. It will not sufficiently narrow and focus the improvement outcomes of the school (Geoff Masters).[18]

In schools, it is not always simple to identify the outcomes by which achievement of the purpose can be measured. There are so many complexities of input and process that it is tempting to identify quite abstract outcomes such as this: 'every student achieving the best possible outcomes for themselves'. However, while statements of this type might properly form part of the vision and purpose, they are not tangible enough to be outcomes.

As a rule, if an outcome cannot be detected in some way, then it is not precise enough to be used. Schools without defined outcomes can never 'fail', but they can't 'succeed' either!

That does not mean that schools can only limit themselves to outcomes that can be measured numerically. Nor does it mean that every outcome area *should* be measured.

A well-balanced approach would be to choose and benchmark a variety of the indicators that are likely to show that the vision and purpose of the school are being achieved, and then persevere with those indicators.

Some of the obvious indicators might be:
o 'Results data' – especially in those areas that the school is emphasising through its curriculum and pedagogy.
o Scores on comparative tests.
o Indicators of student engagement.
o Anecdotal reports about student attitudes to and ownership of their own learning.
o Surveys of staff, student and parent satisfaction.
o Enrolment trends.
o Action research studies, perhaps conducted in conjunction with a tertiary institution.
o Comparative snapshots over time.
o Collegial walk-throughs at thoughtful intervals, with the collegial group focusing on observable indicators.
o Results of evaluative data created by the employing system.

o   Use of consultancy services to assist with any of these processes.

Not just the system generated data!

There are good reasons for being cautious about relying too much on indicators such as results in annual tests or high-stakes external exams.

The main drawbacks of these indicators are that the time-lapse is long and the input variables are hard to quantify. Although indicators such as National Tests or Annual Surveys form one dimension of outcome measurement, they are most valuable when they are used to track the performance of individual students over time. Schools and teachers have access to much more immediate data if they are willing to systematically use the information that is readily available through classroom tasks and tests.

Creating outcome systems based upon every teacher monitoring day-to-day results, academic performance and student engagement, and then using these as feedback to improve the learning process, will be far more 'nimble' and powerful than 'after-the-fact' analysis of National Tests.

Finally
Outcome goals (like all goals) should be '**SMART**'.
In this context, the SMART acronym should be slightly adapted to represent the following aspects of effective school goals:

Specific – They should be related to distinct and distinguishable elements of student, staff or school performance.

Measurable – The particular outcomes can be measured in some way. Obviously, this is easiest when the outcome is numerical, but qualitative as well as quantitative information is also valid, so long as a way of determining improvements can be agreed.

Amenable to Action – The people who will address these outcomes can influence the indicators chosen. For example, although school-wide data is influenced by the outcomes achieved by every teacher, the connection is not sufficiently direct to engage many staff.

Realistic – While ambitious vision is to be encouraged, if the stretch goals that result are too far removed from the present reality, staff may be easily discouraged by apparent slow progress. In these cases, more realistic interim goals are the best way to support optimistic engagement.

Time-framed – The outcomes should be achievable within the time-frame of the planning period. Once again, this is psychologically important, as well as being clear and logical.

There are many processes for identifying appropriate outcomes. The three included in the 'Technical Manual' are usually both effective and enjoyable:

1. 'The forensic evidence approach.'
2. 'Mapping from the intentions.'
3. 'Cause for celebration.'

Constructing The Values Frame

Let's revisit the purpose of identifying values in order to sharpen the exploration of this Frame of the 'Window'.

We all have many values. We value things, people and lifestyle features, pets and status. But the context of this conversation about values is relatively narrow. In this Frame, we are searching for agreement on the social and cultural values that will help us to create the ideal learning community within which to pursue our vision for the school.

Because values are often abstractions, they easily become what Chris Argyris[19] describes as 'espoused values'. He uses this term to distinguish them from 'values in action'. The difference is comparable to that between a person who says they believe that charity is important, and one who gives up his Christmas day to work in a homeless shelter.

As Chris Argyris[19] explained in his very insightful writing about leadership behaviours, it is quite common for a person or group to have one model in their heads about what is important, but to actually behave quite a different way. They may have a noble intention, but act in ways that are defensive and self-protective. Because of this, it is essential that the values discussions are very open and explicit, and go as far as identifying the actual behaviours associated with the values the community agrees on.

Gaining agreement at the level of espoused values or abstract principles is easy. Taking the next step to achieve understanding of and commitment to enacted values requires a little more effort.

In creating the Values Frame for our 'Window of Certainty', we are searching for those shared 'values in action' which will guide our behaviours in the school community. These values are deeply cultural. When identified and adopted by all, they transform the ways in which teachers, leaders and students regard each other, communicate with each other and support each other.

Because the nature of education is such that the transmission of values is important, the behaviours we choose in modelling these values matter greatly. Students will learn far more from the principles and values they perceive in their teachers' actions than from anything they *are told* about values.

Because the culture of the school is almost always created by the behaviour and interactions of teachers and leaders, the conversations related to the Values Frame will be initiated at a staff level.

Determining the Values Frame is a two-step exploration:
Step 1
Elicit the values we regard as essential if this community of learners is to thrive.

Step 2
Agree on the behaviours that will demonstrate those values in action.

Among the many possible ways of identifying and exploring the values that we want to embed in the school community, I have included three approaches in the 'Technical Manual' each has a different starting point, though elements of each process overlap:

1. **'Using an open-ended question.'**
2. **'Working from a list of values.'**
3. **'Beginning with behaviours.'**

Constructing The Beliefs Frame

What are beliefs?
It is important to begin with a clear idea of what a belief is. Beliefs are perceptual generalisations we make about ourselves and about the world. They operate as 'rules of thumb' for decision-making. Our most treasured beliefs (the ones that work for us best) become features of our 'quality world', our personal reference point.

All strategies are underpinned by beliefs. When we are trying to be as effective as we can be, our perceptions of how events are caused, or why people behave in a certain way, are critical drivers of the strategies we choose.

We adopt beliefs because we think they will be helpful guides towards success.
*As a teacher, I chose to believe that **all** students could learn and improve the skills I taught as a Physical Education teacher, or the concepts I imparted in the Mathematics classroom. It did not mean that I held the belief that every student could become a competitive sportsperson, or that a*

child with an intellectual disability could master calculus. I knew these extremes were unlikely, but that did not shake my core belief.

I adopted this belief both because I thought it was ethical – 'the right thing to do'. In my view, I had no right to pre-ordain for students the limits of their achievement. I also thought this belief was useful. When I expected continual progress from my students; when I challenged them to be the best they could be, they lived up to that expectation.

When we believe something it 'feels right'. It fits into the story we tell ourselves about how the world is, and what our place in it is.

As professionals in a learning organisation, the beliefs that teachers and leaders should focus on are those that drive effective strategies; those that are useful. It makes no sense to choose beliefs that inhibit our effectiveness.

There is an important sense in which beliefs are largely pragmatic. What would be the sense in clinging to a belief that no longer works for you? By definition, helpful beliefs underpin the ways in which we work effectively.
However, people don't always have a very reliable sense about what works. But in the professional milieu there is more likely to be either consensus, or at least informed discussion, about pedagogical and developmental issues than occurs in non-professional contexts.

The most productive focus is on USEFUL beliefs

The nature of beliefs is such that they either empower or inhibit us. Personally, we are all familiar with unhelpful beliefs about ourselves and the damaging effects that these can have on our focus and our confidence. Conversely, we know that helpful beliefs have a significant effect in creating positive and optimistic attitudes.

Because all beliefs are choices (they only _seem_ like truths), they can be changed. They do change: with experience; with new information; through the influence of others; or through our experience of a belief as 'un-useful'.

Dr Albert Mamary[20] urged his audiences to "**Choose useful beliefs!**" It is crucial to choose beliefs that support our goals; convey our values; promote our future vision; channel our sense of purpose; and lead to success.

Two footnotes about assumptions and attitudes:
1. Assumptions are tacit beliefs – insidious because they are often unconscious and unspoken. When beliefs are openly discussed and evaluated, these tacit beliefs are also challenged. Like attitudes (which are habitual perceptions) they are not used to being challenged, so the beliefs conversations are often profoundly uncomfortable – but all the more necessary because of that. As all of these belief-related perceptions are powerful filters of both possibility and necessity (but are usually outside our awareness), addressing them **overtly** enables the school community to speak candidly about matters that have a powerful impact on behaviour.
2. Because all beliefs, assumptions and attitudes act as 'self-fulfilling prophecies', we usually think there is evidence for our beliefs. When we believe something to be true, we filter the information coming through our perceptual system to verify that belief. This is another reason for candidly examining our beliefs and assumptions, and for taking action to question their usefulness.

We don't all have to believe the same things about everything. This would be impossible. Between us, we would have to address hundreds of different beliefs, all driven by the different life experiences of the participating staff.

What we do have to discuss are important beliefs about: how and why people are motivated; about learning and teaching; and about the most productive way to present and manage curriculum.

Framing the beliefs conversation:
It is helpful when identifying shared beliefs to set the discussion in a frame. This helps everyone to find a reference for 'useful beliefs'.

Two ways to do this are examined in the 'Technical Manual' pages.
They are:
1. 'Through open-ended questions.'
2. The 'list' or 'paired alternatives' approach.

Other processes for reaching consensus on beliefs are also suggested.

CHAPTER TEN

What do you risk without a 'Window of Certainty'?

Most people have worked in a school, or another organisation, where the defining expectations and limits of personal freedoms are not made explicit. In such places, the expectations and assumptions of the leaders are only revealed by exception. We find out where the boundaries are when we trip over them!

This is not a very efficient or effective way to find what is expected or allowed. Even more unproductive is the reaction of those people who discover 'after the fact' that they have stepped over an invisible boundary. The feedback they receive almost always generates resentment and defensiveness, because limits encountered in this way usually seem capricious and inconsistent.

Even when this is not made explicit, in every organisation there are acceptable and unacceptable behaviours, things that are ok to do or say and those that are not. Finding out what is approved and what is frowned upon only through painful encounters is not fun!

In my first school as a young teacher, I learned many of the boundaries from the Deputy Principal's interventions. On many occasions, he came storming into my classroom to reprimand my students and even drag them off to be caned. (It was seen as OK to hit students back then!) This was always accompanied by a glare at me and a muttered: "I'll talk to YOU later!" I dreaded those talks. His anger almost blistered the paintwork!

Of course, I did learn where some boundaries were. He was particularly clear that students were not allowed to talk to each other or to be out of their seats. I soon learned not to set cooperative tasks!

In the long year that I worked at that school, I came to realise with horror that bullying of all kinds was regarded as appropriate in order to subdue the students. Achieving order and compliance was far more important than how it was achieved, or the educational objectives it was supposed to support. Learning was rarely discussed.

Of course, I left as soon as I could. Although there was unity and energy among small pockets of staff, it was never allowed to flourish.

Hopefully, the different approaches in most schools of today are not so clearly delineated. However, contradictions are not hard to find. Schools that trumpet 'caring and nurturing for all' in their vision statement, but strategically marginalise failing students do exist. That contradiction is not usually discussed. There are also many examples of teachers in the same school who agree on the importance of 'respect', but whose values-in-action behaviours make it clear that they mean very different things by this value. Each fumes at the other's interpretation, and collegiality is impaired. The open discussion that would lead to unity rarely occurs.

According to Marco Korn:[21] "One of the main causes for destructive and entrenched conflict in workplaces is the perception by one person or group that their objectives and/or values are under threat by someone else.

Additionally, it is assumed that this is the deliberate intention of the other party. This is a common scenario."

Every contradiction and conflict of this kind that remains unresolved creates uncertainty and damages cohesion in the school. The energy of teachers is diffused by the resulting doubts or discomfort. In these circumstances, the effectiveness of teacher collaboration is diminished, there is often a sense that 'we are on our own' and there is a general diffidence among teachers and students about what is important and worth pursuing. When we don't talk about what we are doing together and why; what works and does not; what counts as success; or how we should treat each other; we are all left guessing.

Eliminating these enigmas is powerful. It is also efficient and effective. The conversations that lead to clarity about the 'Window of Certainty' are BIG conversations with far-reaching consequences.

- Section 2 -

The 'Window of Certainty 'Technical Manual'

This section describes, in some detail, processes for reaching agreement about the 'Window of Certainty'.

Many participants in our workshops have asked for more specific information about how to work with their colleagues to create a "Window of Certainty' in their school. This 'Technical Section' is for them, and for anyone else who would like to be very systematic about creating their 'Window'.

The eleven processes listed are my attempts to describe the steps you might need to follow if you are leading a large school. They are not riveting reading because I have tried to include enough detail for an inexperienced facilitator to follow them. Of course, if your context is a small or less complex school or team, you will have less need for elaborate processes.

The processes below are mostly described as if these conversations are being conducted between teachers. However, with some modification, they are suitable discussion processes for older class groups and parent groups as well.

CHAPTER ELEVEN

Creating the Vision

11.1

'Collaborative Vision Creation':

A collaborative process with 9 steps.

(Not all of these steps will always be necessary. Be guided by the degree of consensus that exists as the process develops).

This method begins the process of creating a vision from scratch. It is a strategy that can be used when the leader believes that starting from scratch and building the vision through overtly collaborative process is essential for building community consensus.

It embraces the complexity involved in such a process. The roles of many individuals in the school are such that they can only envision the future in their own area. Everyone can make a contribution, but the collective inputs will need careful synthesis before they constitute a common vision.

If this method is chosen, the wider perspective of the executive leader must be applied sensitively throughout the process, both to shape and to collect the ideas of others, and to help them 'zoom out' to the bigger picture.

The process begins with a reflection on what is best about the school as it is at present, and then uses this as the launch-pad for a question that will help the participants 'zoom out' into a preferred future. Some examples of such questions are offered below (in step b.), but it is best to design your own.

Step A – individual reflect on the school's present strengths:

Working individually:
Each person writes down what they see as the most important accomplishments and most effective practices of the school as they perceive it at present.

If it is appropriate, some group discussion and sharing can follow this step.

Step B – still working individually:

Each individual then writes one or two headlines, each with a few lines of a newspaper story about the school five years in the future. The story describes significant success the school has had.
OR Each person describes the school, as they would like it

to be in five years time, either in words or with pictures. **OR** Each person imagines himself or herself as a highly successful graduate of the future school; a person who is happy, fulfilled, responsible and respected. They write down the ways in which the school was able to help them to become this person.

Step C - In small groups:

Share stories, and develop a list of common vision themes to use as a basis for writing a Vision Statement. The executive leader makes sure that everyone understands the need for 'big picture' themes to emerge.

Step D - Working individually again, but sitting in a circle:

Without discussion, each person writes his or her own version of a Vision Statement on a sheet of paper for 2-5 minutes. Each then passes their paper on to their neighbour. The neighbour underlines the key words and phrases they like best. The statements are then passed on to the next person, who underlines the key words and phrases they like best. Repeat until everyone has seen (and underlined) everyone else's Vision Statement.

This is the point at which to emphasise the need to avoid 'motherhood statements', and to be as specific and as concrete as possible.

Step E

In the small group, create a Vision Statement that would mirror the most frequently occurring underlined themes, phrases and key words.

Step F

The vision created by this group is then circulated among all other groups, (ideally when they are meeting together in one place, but this is not essential). All groups view the visions created by the others, and modify or edit their own.

Step G

Finally, the leadership team (or a team specifically gathered for this process) gathers the input, and uses a consensus process to forge one compact Vision Statement from the inputs.

Step H *(very important)*

The synthesis is returned to all of the participating groups with the question:
"Does this adequately reflect your participation in the process? If not, what is missing?"

Step J

This final round of inputs is returned to the leadership team who will attempt to include any essential elements from the step h. consultation phase.

Their delicate task is to incorporate what will genuinely add to the vision synthesis, but to avoid including minority opinions or making the final document too unwieldy.

The finished document should ideally consist of 4 to 5 sentences at the most.

11.2

An 'Editing the Draft' process:

Use this 5-step process when there is an existing vision, or when the vision is being intentionally re-visited for the purpose of renewal.

Step A

Begin with a reflection on the strengths and most significant accomplishments of the school over the previous 5 years. What are people proud of, both individually and as a community?

If possible, allow opportunities for sharing of these reflections.

Step B

Begin with the existing vision, perhaps with some leadership input, as a draft.

Distribute the draft with a set of questions:
o Does this vision position us well for the future? Will it capture the reasons why students will want to be enrolled here?
o Are the strengths we want to be proud of as a school embodied in this vision?
o Is this vision aligned with our values and beliefs?
o Is this a vision that will appeal to students, parents and teachers?
o Is it simple and easy to understand?
o Is this statement truly aspirational?

o   Does it point to a future to which we all subscribe?

Meeting in small groups, (made up from whatever conversation forums exist around the school - including parents and students), each group will edit the draft and create their own version.

Step C

When all the drafts are in, the Principal or leadership group maps the inputs from across the school and uses a consensus-building approach such as:
- Identifying areas of disagreement or concern.
- Negotiating with the 'Step B' groups to identify meaning.
- Modifying the proposal to generate as much agreement as possible.
- Accepting the most aspirational and optimistic versions to break 'deadlocks'.

Now use steps H and J from the extended visioning process (10.1) to ensure that there is consensus.

Step H

The synthesis is returned to all of the participating groups with the question:
"Does this adequately reflect your participation in the process? If not, what is missing?"

Step J

This final round of inputs is returned to the leadership team, who will attempt to include any essential elements from the consultation phase.

Their delicate task is to include what will genuinely add to the vision synthesis but to avoid making the final document too unwieldy or include a whole lot of minority opinions.

The finished document should ideally consist of four to five sentences at the most.

11.3

'Walking the leader's vision journey':

This abbreviated process is more of a validation process for the leader's vision than a true co-creation. It assumes that the leader (or a leadership group) has created a vision for the school, which they offer to the community as the ideal future for the school.

This strategy is not recommended in most cases. However, it may be the best option when the school community has experienced some turmoil, and is seeking strong leadership to set it in a fresh direction.

To begin this process, the leader consults widely about what is perceived as the past and current strengths and accomplishments of the school.

The leader de-constructs his or her own vision by:
o   Connecting what is robust and desirable about the school (both what is presently happening and what has happened previously) with what he or she believes should be created in the future.

o   Teasing out the process that went into the construction of the new vision; the reason for the different elements of the vision; and the beliefs and values that provide the philosophical foundation of the vision.

He or she then offers each element of the vision to the coalitions of interest that exist in the school, and asks for their inputs in a spirit of genuine enquiry.

The task of the community is to challenge or affirm the elements of the vision, in order to improve it; to contribute to the vision by asking: "Is this the best possible statement of our ideal future?"

Sometimes, leaders hesitate to seek this affirmation of their own reference point for the future because they fear opposition. However, it is actually far better for a leader to face the temporary challenge of robust conversations while seeking consensus on the vision, than to wait for the more prolonged challenges from a divided community when the leader's vision is not understood or owned by others.

Even when this process (the least collaborative of the three) is used, elements of the other processes can be included to increase the level of engagement and involvement.

In particular, **steps H and J**, (from process 9.1) which are used in the more collaborative processes, will ensure that there is a clear validation of the completed vision.

CHAPTER TWELVE

Defining the Outcomes

12.1
'The Forensic Evidence Approach':

Step A

Put this scenario to key groups of students, parents, teachers and community members:

Imagine that in 100 years time, the school's Vision statement is unearthed from a time capsule.

Within the same capsule are other documents and pieces of information, including pictures, items from newsletters and written opinions.

What would you want to see among the pieces of evidence that would prove to you that the school had proudly achieved the goals, targets and lofty intentions that it had set out in the Vision statement?

Step B

As a leadership group, assemble the responses of all of the groups, and sort these responses for common ideas as well as for individual contributions.

Create from these, a synthesis of ten to twelve outcomes that would provide significant evidence of success.

Check to see if these indicators are appropriate ways of addressing the key accountabilities of the school leaders. Unconventional or imaginative options should be seriously considered.

Step C

Publish the set of outcomes that has been put together by the leaders, and ask for community response to these questions:
o   Are these outcomes specific enough so that we will know when we have achieved them?
o   Are they attractive and attainable?
o   Are they challenging enough to encourage us to do our best work?

12.2

'Mapping from the intentions':

This is a slightly more prosaic approach, but a very sound way of ensuring that all the school's aspirational intentions have an outcome test attached to them.

Step A

Create small groups that are led by either teachers or leaders with sound analytic skills.

Each group de-constructs every element of the vision and purpose; (and if values have already been identified, include these as well).

Every implication of the elements that are separated out is considered in this way:
- What will we see and hear in classrooms and around the school?
- What data should change?
- What will students, teachers and parents think or feel that will show this is happening?
- What will we hear being said about the school?

Step B

When every element of the vision and purpose has been mapped to a set of explicit indicators, choose the indicators that will reveal most powerfully that the school has successfully achieved its vision (or is well on the way to doing so).

Step C

Assemble the indicators chosen by each group and share them with every group. All groups process the material, discard any outcomes they regard as invalid, and add any indicators that are now suggested by viewing the ideas of others.

Step D

The leadership group now takes the results of the group processes, and chooses from them the outcomes that will be the most powerful indicators of school success. These should be appropriately challenging but also realistically attainable.

Step E

Publish the reviewed set of outcomes to the community, and invite comments and feedback.

Often, a process of negotiation with the various vested interests in the school is needed at this point. The job of the school leaders is to negotiate in good faith, while ensuring that the outcomes chosen are a suitable match for the vision, and are also a valid expression of success.

12.3

'Cause for celebration':

The emphasis of this process is on identifying steps on the journey, and ways in which to note and celebrate these steps.

Everyone needs to celebrate every step of the way. Waiting until the final destination is achieved can be a very dry and unrewarding business.

Even if other processes are used as the major vehicle for identifying the outcomes, finding reasons to celebrate along the way always feels good.

Step A

Working in groups, participants look for every indicator they can find that the school has taken any step (large or small) towards achieving the vision of excellence it has set itself.

The groups should intentionally look for 'quick wins' – signs that a small step has been taken or a new practice is being attempted.

They should also look for ways in which to identify the progress of new processes or curriculum changes, and tools for measuring these changes.

For example, taking a new teaching practice and chunking it into steps such as:
- Attempted at least once;
- Beginning to include regularly;
- Becoming regular part of my practice;

- Embedded in my practice.

Then the school can use surveys that measure patterns of change in teaching practice to chart progress.

Step B

Create as extensive a list as possible of milestones. Nothing should be too small to include in this list, as long as it is genuinely related to the intentions of the school's vision.

Step C

Decide how to celebrate each milestone. One school I know has put all of its milestones into a huge thermometer, similar to the fundraising thermometers that we often see associated with pleas for contributions to a cause or building renovation. This is a very visible way of charting progress.

This process is probably most powerful when all of the elements of the 'Window of Certainty' have been assembled, as progress within all four Frames can then be identified and acknowledged.

Exploring The Difference It Makes

---CHAPTER THIRTEEN---

Agreeing the Values

13.1

'Using an open-ended question':

Step A

Working in small groups of staff, use one of the following possible key questions, or frame one for yourself along the same lines:

"What values should be embodied in the way we treat each other, if we are going to get the best from each other?"
Or

"Which are the values to which we should all aspire in order to make this school a great place to work; a happy place where students learn to be great human beings as well as successful scholars?"
Or (focusing on behaviours)
"How will leaders, teachers and students behave towards each other when this school has become the best possible place in which to teach and learn? What values are associated with these behaviours?"

Choosing the right question to ask is important.
If the school is to thrive and provide the best quality of education for each student, then the question must be asked in a way that encourages noble and growth-focused values.

Record the values on post-it notes.

Step B

Translating the identified values into values in action.

First ask the groups (or the whole staff working together) to arrange the post-it notes so that similar values are sorted into similar categories.

Individually (or in pairs) ask people to write on index cards the behaviours that would be examples of each different value if it were seen in action in the school. Put the value as a heading, and the list the behaviours below.
It may be useful for them to identify:
- What they would see students doing;

- What they would see teachers doing;
- What they would see leaders doing.

If Step 1 generated many different values, identify who will work on which group of values.

People often seem to agree on values in the abstract, but expressions of value often mean different things to different people. Therefore this step can be very illuminating!

Look out for discrepancies between the meanings of values. For example, some teachers believe respect = obedience (deference in one direction only), while others equate it with mutual (two-way) regard between people. Working out different perceptions such as these is intrinsic to achieving a 'Window of Certainty' that will usefully guide behaviour in the school.

Remind participants in the conversation that the main issue is to identify the behaviours that will contribute to the school culture that they want to create.

Step C

Sort the cards and display them in a staffroom or common meeting place where they can be easily viewed. It is often useful to leave them on display for a week or so to allow everyone to reflect on them.

When the staff returns to the activity, ask people (working in pairs) to identify value cards that they perceive as 'essentially in agreement' with regard to behaviours, and then categorise them according to similarities.

Anyone can challenge, or say that they want to add to an identified category. However, when this activity occurs, there is usually broad consensus about many of the values categories and the associated behaviours.

Step D

Initiate a *pair, four, eight* process for each of the values where there is disagreement about behaviours.
Pairs work together to come to an agreement about the importance of the value and how it will look in action. They then join another pair to negotiate agreement in a group of 4; and so on, until consensus is reached about whether the value should be included, and what it will mean in terms of behaviour.

This sounds like a long process, but it is often surprisingly quick, except where there is **significant** disagreement about whether a value should be included or what it means in action.

In such cases, it is the leaders' responsibility to make a decision about where the consensus lies, and to ask those who disagree to go along with what most staff seem to believe is right.

Ask every staff member to make a commitment to living these values in action in their work.

Step E
Publish the agreed values as the Left Frame of the 'Window of Certainty'.
Publish the behaviours that have been associated with these values around the school - and also in the school community.

13.2

'Working from a list of values':

Step A

There are multiple possible starting points for this process.

Start with a list of aspirational values.

Lists of common educational values are easily accessible. This one is from a NSW Education web site:
Integrity, excellence, respect, responsibility, cooperation, participation, care, fairness, democracy.

Another list from a social/educational context is:
Accountability, Achievement, Autonomy, Success, Belonging, Care for others, Education, Empathy, Faith, Fairness, Generosity, Good relationships, Justice, Learning, Respect for others, Recognition of difference, Responsibility, Certainty, Self-worth, Service, Tradition.

The drawback with lists like these is that they are framed in the very abstract way that leads to them being easily 'espoused', but only translated into action with a great deal of work.

Another starting point might be:

Using 'personal' professional values as a starting point.

Ask everyone to share his or her most cherished professional values, and use these as a starting point.
Or

Elicit values from parents and discuss with teachers.

Parents almost always have positive aspirational values for their children, so this is another possible starting point for this phase of the conversation.

Step B

Ask a question that will focus attention on the usefulness of the value in creating a positive supportive culture.

"Which of these values are most helpful in guiding the way we treat each other, if we are going to get the best from each other?"
Or
"Which of these values should we aspire to in order to make this school a great place to work, and a happy place where students learn to be great human beings as well as successful scholars?"

Use the *sticker dots* process to identify the values that teachers believe are most important in creating a positive, supportive culture.

In this process post all of the values identified through Step A on a board or display them on sheets of paper. Each person is give 6 to 8 adhesive dots (available from all newsagents) which they attach beside side the values they think most helpful for creating the culture that will underpin the vision for the school.

The consensus is usually plainly visible from the placement of the dots.

Step C

In small groups, write on separate pages descriptions of the behaviours that will match each of the values identified. There should be at least one descriptor per value, and they must illustrate related actions and interactions that are desirable for creating a helpful culture.

Now use a process I call 'pass the propositions'. Circulate the pages authored by each group to the other groups, so that every group has a chance to view and edit the behaviours described by others.

As they examine the behaviours associated with each value, they have a choice of three actions:
- Where they agree that the described behaviour matches the value, they give it a green tick ✓.
- If they agree with the description, but want to add to the descriptor (in the same spirit as the original), they place a green tick ✓ and add their own words.
- If they think there is a preferred behaviour (or a set of behaviours) that will better exemplify the value in action, they put a red cross ✗ by the original and write their own preferred descriptors.

Step D
When the papers have all been circulated, extract those values where the contributions of every group indicate that there is consensus about the behaviours associated with those values.
Publish these.

The next task is to work with the values that have been identified, but about which there is disagreement concerning what they mean in practice. There will not usually be many of these after the previous rounds of process.

Ask each group to look at the statements from 6 perspectives:
- Teachers considering what they want from students.
- Students considering what they want from teachers.
- Teachers considering what they want from colleagues.
- Leaders considering what they want from teachers.
- Teachers considering what they want from leaders.
- Parents considering what they want from teachers and leaders.

If there is conflict between the perspectives, resolve the question by asking which behaviours will be seen as congruent with the value from most perspectives.

When consensus emerges, publish the list of values in the Values Frame of the 'Window', and display the list of associated behaviours in every classroom.

13.3

'Beginning with behaviours':

Step A

Working in pairs, list the behaviours that are likely to lead to a need-satisfying, happy, productive school community. Staff should write these from a personal perspective, but also from the perspective of happy students who are learning well.

Collate the contributions, which often will look something like this.
o *Listening to each other with understanding.*
o *Respecting each other's opinions.*
o *Supporting and encouraging each other's efforts.*
o *Being a friendly presence for each other.*
o *Trusting each other and being worthy of trust.*
o *Participating fully in our work.*
o *Helping each other whenever possible.*
o *Asking for help when we need it.*
o *Taking responsibility for the things that are ours to do.*
o *Respecting and appreciating our differences.*
o *Learning and using the courtesies that are important to each other.*
o *Optimising the achievements of both students and teachers.*

Group all the 'like' items.

The advantage of a list like this is that it translates relatively easily into values-in-action - the actual behaviours we would see if the value were being modelled. However, there is still some work to do.

Step B

Use a sticker dot process to identify the behaviours that are seen as most important (described in detail in process 12.2)

Post the list of behaviours. Then give everyone 6 stickers to post alongside the behaviours they think are most helpful for creating the culture that will underpin the vision for the school.

List all the behaviours that a significant number of the staff has identified as most important.

Allow all those who voted for behaviours that seemed not as important in the consensus round a couple of minutes to explain why these should be added. Give everyone one more sticker to add a vote for these if they now see them as important.

Include only one or two of these behaviours in your list.

Step C

For each behaviour on the completed list, ask the pairs of staff to drill a little more deeply using these questions:
- "What difference would it make if everyone were behaving like this?"
- "What would we **not** see happening if everyone were committed to the associated value?"
- "Can we 'universalise' the importance of this behaviour - does it benefit everyone in the school?"

- "How will it make the school a happier and more productive place?"

When they have answered these questions, enquire further:

1. "How will we name the <u>value</u> associated with the behaviour we want to see?"
2. "What is the full description of that value in action?"

Step D

Either a volunteer group of staff, or the leadership group, collates all the inputs, and then lists the identified values with an associated description of that value in action.

Circulate the results of that collation, and ask for further inputs. Incorporate these into the final product.

Publish the list of values in the Values Frame of the 'Window of Certainty', and display the list of associated behaviours in every classroom and staffroom.

CHAPTER FOURTEEN

Choosing Useful Beliefs

14.1

'The open-ended question approach.'

Step A
Work in small groups or pairs.
The groups address some suitable open-ended questions that match the school context and the level of development of the other Frames of the 'Window of Certainty'.
Some examples might be:

Possible question 1:
"If this is our vision, what beliefs should we have in common to underpin the work we do together?"

Exploring The Difference It Makes

Use this frame if you already have a school vision or statement of purpose, but have not teased out the underpinning beliefs.

Possible question 2:
"If we assume that we aspire to provide the best possible learning and growth for every student in our school, what beliefs would we have to share to underpin that work?"
Use this frame if you are building a framework of beliefs as part of the process of creating a vision and refining the school's purpose.

Possible question 3:
"Imagine that, in 5 years' time, we will look back at today and reflect that this was the time when we adopted new beliefs, which took us to a whole new level of professional achievement: What would those new beliefs have been?"
(Use this question if you have a thriving school, but would like to drive the performance of the school to an even higher level).

Possible Question 4:
"What do research, experience and expert practice tell us are useful beliefs on which to base our strategies?"

Each group identifies a set of beliefs that they believe is important for the school. Limit each group to 5 or 6 beliefs.

Step B

When each group has identified a set of important beliefs, they ask themselves (about each belief statement in turn): "What difference in practice will this belief make?"
1. Is it useful for:
    o Suggesting strategies that will encourage students?

o Helping us understand how to manage student behaviour in ways that encourage learning?
  o Underpinning teaching strategies that optimise learning for all students?
2. "What evidence can we offer for the usefulness of this belief - drawing on our own reservoir of experience, and on research findings or 'best practice' models?"
3. "Could this belief be limiting?"

Encourage participants to write, doodle and draw key ideas on a large sheet of paper to illustrate and enhance the discussion.

Step C

Conduct a 'teacher belief exchange' (using a collaborative 'jig-saw' approach)

In this phase of conversation:
o One person should remain in their own group as the 'source', while the others become 'ambassadors of meaning' and join each of the other groups. The ambassadors carry key ideas, themes and questions from the initial conversation into their new conversations.
o The groups welcome the 'ambassadors' and briefly share the main ideas, themes and questions of the initial conversation. Encourage ambassadors to link and connect ideas arising from their previous conversations - listening carefully and building on each other's contributions.
o By the end of the second round, all of the groups will be 'cross-pollinated' with insights from prior conversations.

Step D

o   Participants should return to their home (original) group to synthesise their discoveries. A new question that helps deepen the exploration is posed for this fourth round of conversation: "If we are to be our very best, which beliefs should we adopt for the future?"
o   During this fourth round of conversation, encourage the sharing of personal insights into discoveries that participants have made about their own about beliefs, self-talk and visualisation, as well as strategic insights.
o   In this final round of the conversation, dig deeply for patterns that can be identified, new collective knowledge and the best belief statements to take forward.

Each group then writes a report or communiqué that is presented to the leadership group.

Step E

The leadership group extracts the consensus of the staff about which beliefs will be most useful in advancing the school's vision and achieving the desired outcomes.

Where there is clearly dissent about some beliefs that the leaders believe are important, they undertake whatever research is necessary to provide critical information to the staff.

There is no shortcut to this process – it can take quite a long time. But the ongoing conversation will continue to build alignment and clarity about values in the school.

The beliefs on which consensus is achieved are published. Those on which there is still debate are subjected to one or more of the processes suggested at 13.3

14.2

'Using a List of Paired Alternatives'

Step A

Present a list that is a series of paired alternatives, as below. The pairs of beliefs you will choose should be specific to your school. It should address the beliefs that underpin strategies that, in your school, will lead to effective outcomes.

Participating teachers, working individually, underline the beliefs that they share.

- Motivation is internal. The behaviour of staff and children is based on an internal process of choice.
- Motivation is external. Staff and students can be made to do things without a negative impact on their learning and enthusiasm.

- Ability is fixed.
- Ability improves with learning.

- Student learning resilience grows when they have to struggle to find meaning or solve problems.
- Students should never be challenged beyond their current level of confidence and achievement.

- Differentiated teaching means different content and pedagogy for every student.
- Differentiated teaching involves teaching at three levels: teaching those who are ready; extending those who have moved beyond; pre-teaching those who are not yet there.

- Language should always be taught using a phonics approach.
- A mixed approach to language teaching is most effective.

- Students can become independent learners by learning to self-evaluate their work.
- Students can only become independent learners when they have reached a certain level.

- Creating good relationships and having a friendly approach is an essential capability for teachers.
- Good relationships are not essential for effective learning.

- Creativity is built upon a foundation of basic skills.
- Creativity can emerge at any level of skill development.

- Every teacher should use exactly the same recommended pedagogies in their classroom.
- Teachers need pedagogical autonomy in order to cater for the learning needs of the students in their class.

This list could go on indefinitely, but does not need to. You will probably have already identified the main 'burning issues' created by divergent beliefs among your staff.

Even more important, the staff and leaders of most schools already know what beliefs conversations are important through observing the variety of strategic practices that are evident in the classrooms of the school.

It's not necessary for teachers to agree about every aspect of their professional practice. Some varied practices, and the beliefs that underpin them, can coexist comfortably. The important judgement for the leaders to make is about which beliefs are critical for continuous improvement of effective teaching practice.

Step B

When there is clear consensus about some beliefs, place them in an 'agreed' category.

Focusing on the beliefs where there is division of opinion, construct a comparison chart for each alternative:

Working in pairs, teachers ask each other:
"What strategies will be supported by each of these compared beliefs?"
Or
"What strategies will each of the paired beliefs lead to in practice?"

When that activity is completed, each teacher pair joins with another to create a group of four, and these groups attempt to achieve consensus.

Each group reports what it can agree on, and recommends these agreed statements of belief to the leadership group (or to a 'beliefs and strategies' working party).

Step C

The leadership group (or working party) extracts from the reports the beliefs that are generally favoured (or closest to consensus) from the group recommendations.
They add to these the beliefs on which there was already consensus after Step 1.

These are published in the Beliefs Frame of the 'Window', and the strategies that follow from each belief are identified in a briefing paper to staff.

Where there is clearly lack of consensus about some beliefs, the members of the leadership group (or working party) undertake whatever research is necessary to provide relevant information to the staff. (New information can often change beliefs). In order to achieve consensus, the process leader can then revisit one of the procedures previously described.

Important Note:
Simply forging ahead without consensus about beliefs is usually counter-productive.

When teachers are asked to adopt a particular strategy (a pedagogical practice or a curriculum process), but do not accept the underlying belief system, they often use the strategy ineffectively. There is too much intrinsic contradiction for teachers when they attempt to implement a strategy that depends for its success on one belief, while they actually believe something else.

For example, teachers who believe that external control is both possible and desirable will not effectively use internal control strategies. They will use the strategies of internal control as if they were a means of controlling the students, instead of influencing the students to exercise self-control.

When the internal control strategy fails to achieve student compliance, frustration sets in for the teachers who continue to believe that they *should* be able to (and *ought* to) 'control' the students. Consequently, these teachers revert to external control strategies.

Similar situations will occur when teachers are asked to encourage independent learning, but personally believe that only highly capable students are able to learn independently.

A mismatch between beliefs and strategies is almost always counterproductive. Leaders who want their schools to flourish will always persist in encouraging teachers to use the most useful beliefs.

14.3

Other processes

The following processes can be used to explore other issues or disagreement that arises from the beliefs conversation. :

1. When there is a 'knowledge issue', provide training or skilling programmes that will enable teachers to make more informed decisions.
2. Use 'case studies' of events in the school to examine or challenge beliefs.
3. Observe patterns of behaviour and language among teachers, parents or students, and then elicit the belief systems that underpin them.
4. Present dilemmas based on problematic school situations.
5. Conduct a PMI (Plus, Minus, Interesting) on the usefulness of particular beliefs.
6. Analyse strategies that are generally known to be effective, and elicit the aligned values/beliefs.

7. Discuss the underpinning educational philosophy from work programs, curriculum programs, national teacher standards etc.
8. Initiate provocative statements about one or more beliefs.

CHAPTER FIFTEEN

An example of a completed 'Window of Certainty'

An example of a completed 'Window of Certainty' from *Enterprise Road High School* is provided on the next page.

It is accompanied by these explanatory notes, especially the 'values in action', which are so important to ensuring that there is clarity about the meaning of many values and beliefs.

Explanatory notes for the *Enterprise Road HS* 'Window':

Vision:
Our vision is expected to be a set of stretch goals. There was debate over such things as: "All Students ... will aspire to personal excellence." But what sense would it make to write: "93% of our students will aspire ..."? Our dream would be for all of them to aspire greatly, so we have said so.

Outcomes:
We have chosen 5 outcomes: a mixture of results data and surveys. It is not necessary to measure everything we do.

Values:
Our 'values in action' are:

Positive care and concern for everyone: We expect that leaders and teachers will always look after the well-being of their students and their colleagues, in the same way that they care for themselves. Whenever a student or teacher is

Exploring The Difference It Makes

Our Vision:
High Expectations; Supportive Relationships; Quality Outcomes.
In this learning community all students will:
- Have the opportunity and encouragement to succeed;
- Aspire to personal excellence in all dimensions of education;
- Achieve the best results they are capable of;
- Thrive in our safe, supportive and inspiring ethos.

We Value:
- Positive care and concern for everyone;
- Warm, Respectful and Courteous Behaviour;
- The availability of coaching and support;
- High expectations of the students and of each other;
- Collaboration, interdependence, teamwork and cooperation;
- Acceptance of diversity;
- Personal Creativity and innovation;
- Teaching excellence;
- Celebration of all improvements;.
- Joyful Classrooms.

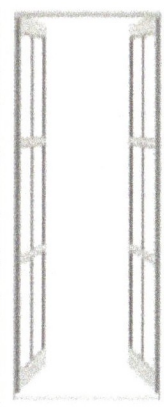

Outcomes:
1. Data shows that academic outcomes improve constantly for every student.
2. All students report when surveyed that they feel safe, supported and engaged.
3. All students believe their teachers have high expectations of them.
4. Exit and Alumni surveys show that the % of students leaving the school to enter further training and employment increases annually.
5. The school enrolment grows each year.

Our Beliefs:
Responsibility, control and motivation come from the inside;
All people can learn, and value learning and change;
Teachers are 'warm demanders';
Our leaders' primary role is to lead the learning and improve student outcomes;
Teachers make a difference to the aspirations and outcomes of students;
Good relationships are the foundation of effective teaching and learning;
Effective feedback must be embedded in formative evaluation;
It is necessary and acceptable to make mistakes when learning;
All teachers adopt known exemplary practices in teaching and learning;
Everyone in this school learns and practises self-evaluation;
Resilience improves when students know how to improve;
Teachers who know their students well teach them well;
Outcomes are improved when students understand the Criteria and Standards on which work is assessed;

facing difficulty or is distressed, help will be available to enable them to meet the challenge.

Warm, respectful and courteous behaviour: teachers, parents and students all extend this approach to each other in words and actions. In particular, as teachers we are committed to model this in the way we behave with students and parents.

The availability of coaching and support: this availability is embedded in systems that enable teachers and students to access coaching and support whenever they are required. Parents are also able to access these services.

High expectations of students and of each other: high expectations are always balanced with capability-building. While it is the students' job to do their very best, it is the teachers' job to be sure they know how to achieve this. Teachers also hold each other to expectations of teaching excellence.

Collaboration, interdependence, teamwork and cooperation: making time to share, plan and learn together is a priority for teachers and leaders. This is our main instrument for reducing 'within-school variation'. The more frequently and freely we share our strengths, the more capable we will be.

Acceptance of Diversity: we know that everyone is not the same, so we value responsible autonomy rather than uniformity. By sharing our varied talents as teachers, we are helping each other to cater for the diversity of students' learning needs.

Personal Creativity and Innovation: these thrive when autonomy is encouraged, but are stunted by expectations of conformity. As teachers, we allow our students freedom to demonstrate learning in distinctive ways; as leaders, we structure our systems so that they cater for teacher creativity.

Teaching excellence: the evidence that there are effective and ineffective teaching strategies is compelling. As leaders and teachers, we are committed to draw from reliable research in order to continually extend our skills and capabilities.

Celebration of all improvements: as we work to make the learning of students and the expertise of teachers more visible, we will create systems to sharpen our awareness of even small improvements - and celebrate them extravagantly!

Joyful classrooms: The Positive Psychology Movement shows that both students and teachers are more likely to learn, and to perform more effectively, when they are having fun. We will never be so busy that we don't have time for laughter and enjoyment.

Beliefs:

Not all of our beliefs require explanation: the strategies they drive are obvious in most cases. However, a few points are highlighted:

Internal Control and Motivation: The belief that internal motivation and control underpin human behaviour pervades all of our strategies. The destructive effects of trying to control others and provide external motivation are well-documented. Although we are prepared to set limits to personal freedom and impose consequences if necessary, we know that 'penalties' do not change behaviour. When a behaviour is inappropriate, it is always our job to teach a 'better way'.

Expert teaching and learning: evidence-based practice is the foundation of teaching and learning at our school. The work of Marzano[22], Hattie[23] and William[24] informs many of our teaching beliefs and practices. If there is evidence of a 'best way' to do things, why would we choose second best? At the same time, we always recognise that teaching is an art, in which the artists' job is to constantly monitor the impact of their art, and modify it creatively to help students to achieve optimally.

Feedback, Self-Evaluation, Criteria and Standards: When students know what they need to do to succeed; have opportunities to improve; can evaluate their own work, and have access to explicit teaching and supportive coaching, they are empowered to take responsibility for their own achievements. This is not just an immediate emancipation - it is also the key to life-long resilience and success!

NOTES

[1] Edward L. Deci with Richard Flaste: 'Why we do what we do', Penguin, 1995.
Deci sets out a compelling case for autonomy, personal competence and relationships as the key motivating factors in human behaviour. He argues that the evidence shows that attempting to control people by promising rewards or threatening punishments 'simply does not work'. What is often described as irresponsibility is the normal human response to coercion. When we feel pressured, we are unlikely to change in any meaningful way; we will most likely respond with minimal (and temporary) compliance or with overt resistance. Deci believes that people behave most responsibly when those who lead and manage them are 'autonomy-supportive'; and that it is when we are freed to be ourselves that we are both most authentic and most effective.

[2] Dr. William Glasser MD: 'Choice Theory – a New Psychology of Personal Freedom', Harper, 1998.
Dr. Glasser was the developer and advocate of the internal psychology that he called Choice Theory. His work is carried on today by the William Glasser Institute of which Judy Hatswell and I are Faculty members. Glasser was one of the pioneers of positive psychology, and his ideas about human behaviour and motivation, and his teaching that people are internally controlled, put him at odds with the mainstream psychology community. Today, the revelations of cognitive neuroscience, the work of researchers such as Deci, and the rise of the psychology movement have validated many of Glasser's insights. However, it is still the case that many leaders and managers (as well as parents and teachers) believe that they can, and should, control the behaviour of other people. As Dr. Glasser repeatedly observed, this erroneous belief results in a great deal of human misery and the failure of many relationships. In the context of this

book, the importance of creating an environment in which teachers and students are encouraged to be autonomously responsible underpins the rationale for the 'Window of Certainty'.

3 Edward L. Deci and R. M. Ryan: 'Intrinsic motivation and self-determination in human behavior', Plenum NY, 1985.

4 *My assertion that there is common ground in identifying 'the needs of the mind' is based on the work of the five influential authors and researchers I refer to below. Although many analysts have focused on the differences between the theories of these authors, the degree of overlap between the ideas is striking:*
- Marylene Gagne and Edward L. Deci: 'Self-Determination Theory and Work Motivation', Journal of Organizational Behaviour, 2005.
- Dr. William Glasser MD: 'Choice Theory – a New Psychology of Personal Freedom', Harper, 1998.
- Daniel H. Pink: '*Drive:* 'The Surprising Truth About What Motivates Us', Cannongate, 2010.
- Abraham H. Maslow: 'A Theory of Human Motivation', Psychological Review, 1943.
- Victor Frankl: 'Man's Search for Meaning', first published as 'From Death Camp to Existentialism', 1943.

Deci lists the needs as competence, relatedness and authority. Glasser expands this to Power (Achievement) Freedom, Relationships and Fun (learning). Pink itemises the needs as Autonomy, Mastery and Purpose. Maslow argues for belonging, self-esteem (achievement), independence (autonomy) and self-actualisation (achieving personal potential). Finally, Victor Frankl emphasises the importance of 'meaning' (living a purposeful existence), as well as achievement, loving relationships and personal autonomy.

Although Glasser is the only one of the five to place learning among the human needs, his recognition of the nexus between fun and learning is insightful and biologically sound. Learning, which is indisputably a necessity for humans, clearly belongs among the needs. Fun is (as Glasser writes) the metabolic pay-off for learning. When we learn something, a gratifying injection of dopamine is the reward!

The suggestion by Frankl (the search for meaning) and Maslow (self-actualisation) that we need to be engaged in something we see as significant and consequential is echoed by Pink, who argues that it is commitment to a cause larger than ourselves that drives the deepest motivation.

5 David Rock: 'SCARF in 2012: Updating the Social Neuroscience of Collaborating with Others, Neuroleadership Journal, Vol Four 2012.
David Rock's SCARF model provides a thoughtful explanation of the reaction of the emotional brain to any perception of threat. It is recommended reading for anyone who teaches, leads or manages people!

6 Richard M.Ryan and Richard Koestner - Research described in E. L. Deci: 'Why We Do What We Do' Penguin, 1995 Ch3.
This research confirms what many of us know from experience; being controlled is inimical to intrinsic motivation, but people respond well to working within limits that are established in an autonomy-supportive manner. In this research, the limits were set by negotiation, and the result was greater acceptance of responsibility, but with no diminution of autonomy.

7 *I can't remember when, and from whom, I first heard this metaphor, but I know I have always attributed it to Barnes Boffey. It originally made powerful sense to me as an educator working with teenagers. It makes even more sense to me in my work with adults.*

8 FutureShape Consulting is the Leadership Development, Coaching and Consulting business founded by the author (Rob Stones). www.futureshape.com.au

9 Victor E. Frankl: 'Man's Search for Meaning', originally published 1959. Recent editions published by Random House.
Frankl's account of his survival in the WW2 Concentration Camps is the background to his belief that mankind is "ultimately self-determining." He wrote that "Man does not simply exist, but

always decides what his next existence will be, what he will become in the next moment."

[10] Peter F Drucker: 'Managing in a Time of Great Change', 1985.
This quote was made famous by Mark Fields of the Ford Motor Company, who attributed it to Drucker in a 2006 article. It quickly morphed into other versions such as 'Culture beats strategy for lunch'. Drucker did not intend to demean strategy (and nor do I). What Drucker was explaining was that, without a receptive culture, or without taking into account the prevailing culture, many strategies do not prosper.

[11] Chris Argyris and Donald Schön: 'Theory in practice: Increasing professional effectiveness', Jossey-Bass 1974, and Chris Argyris: 'Making the undiscussable and its undiscussability discussable', Public Administration Review, 40(3), 1980.
The insights of Argyris and his colleagues explain the endlessly fascinating observation that people's actions and their stated beliefs are frequently contradictory. In studying the behaviour of managers over many years, Argyris realised that when the plans of people who are apparently smart are thwarted in some way, they rarely learn from that experience. Instead, they tend to focus on who (other than themselves) or what (other than their actions) caused the failure – and learn nothing. Yet most of these same people would justify their actions by appealing to apparently rational grounds for their behaviour. Argyris attributed this to the fact that people carry not only a rational set of models in their head (the way they like to see themselves behaving), but also a more automated, unconscious and emotional set of behaviour patterns which are largely made up of defensive and self-protective actions.

[12] Robert A Burton: "On Being Certain: Believing you are right even when you're not', St Martin's Press, 2008.
Robert Burton argues that our 'feeling certain' about something is a mental sensation rather than evidence of any fact! He examines the idea that 'we know something' through mental deliberation or careful evaluation of previous experiences, and explains that our feeling of ''knowing' is not reasoned, but

instead is explained by the way our nervous system operates. The book is controversial, and is a wonderful antidote to the stubborn certainty that brooks no argument.

[13] Dr. Albert Mamary: 'Creating the Ideal School', Rowman and Littlefield, 2007.
I had the pleasure of meeting Al Mamary on several occasions when he visited Australia. His engaging addresses and warm personality created a lasting impact, and his ideas influenced a great deal of my own thinking. Al was well-known for his powerful way of saying important things with disarming simplicity. I can still visualise him - a look of sorrowful perplexity on his face - asking: "Why would you choose useless beliefs?" and exhorting his audience to "Choose useful beliefs!" - it is one of my favourite memories of him.

[14] Marco Korn: 'Conversations for Alignment', www.marcokorn.com.
Marco is an insightful Brisbane-based Psychologist who first showed me his powerful model 'The Pyramid of Alignment' in 2008. Marco is a specialist in the psychology of workplace disputes, and his writing and clear diagrams illustrate how conversations about meaning and purpose tend to unite people in the workplace. He just as clearly shows that a leader's worst enemy is telling people 'how to do the job' (or micro-managing). This approach results in minimal compliance rather than whole-hearted engagement.

[15] V. Robinson, M. Hohepa and C. Lloyd: 'School Leadership and Student Outcomes: Identifying What Works and Why', University of Auckland, 2009.
This study by Viviane Robinson and her colleagues showed that the effect size (on student learning) of 'promoting and participating in Teacher Learning and Development' was twice as great as that for any of the other school leadership behaviours studied.

[16] James M. Kouzes and Barry Z. Posner: 'To Lead, Create a Shared Vision', Harvard Business Review, January 2009.

Kouzes and Posner identify 'Inspiring a Shared Vision' as one of the five exemplary leadership practices. The others are: 'Challenging the Process', 'Enabling Others to Act', 'Modeling the Way' and 'Encouraging the Heart'. The 'Window of Certainty' provides a framework within which all of these practices can flourish. Leaders who are prepared to create the conditions within which their staff can safely express their own autonomy and creativity (while being sure that they are in tune with the vision and purpose of the whole school) give them approval to challenge accepted processes, model, inspire, enable, and encourage.

[17] R.Wageman, D.A. Nunes, J.A. Burrus and J.R. Hackman: 'Senior Leadership Teams', Harvard, 2008.
Wageman and her colleagues argue persuasively that the purpose of a team must be so clear that it creates shared understanding; must be challenging enough to engage the highest level of skills of those involved; and must be consequential enough so that the team believes the energy they expend is worthwhile!

[18] 'The National School Improvement Tool': developed by the Australian Council for Educational Research, 2012.
This instrument incorporates material developed by Professor Geoff Masters for the A.C.E.R. An important recommendation is that the conditions for school improvement include: "Explicit and Clear school-wide targets for improvement, with accompanying timelines." As interpreted by the ACER Consultancy Services, this implies that many schools should 'narrow and sharpen' their improvement agenda in order to make sure that it is clear, explicit and measurable.

[19] Chris Argyris and Donald Schön: 'Theory in practice: Increasing professional effectiveness', Jossey-Bass 1974, and Chris Argyris: 'Making the undiscussable and its undiscussability discussable', Public Administration Review, 40(3), 1980.

[20] Dr. Albert Mamary: 'Creating the Ideal School', Rowman and Littlefield, 2007.

[21] Marco Korn: 'Conversations for Alignment' - www.marcokorn.com

[22] Dr Robert Marzano: 'The Art and Science of Teaching', ASCD, 2007.

[23] Dr John Hattie: 'Visible Learning for Teachers', Routledge, 2012.

[24] Dylan William: 'Embedded Formative Assessment', Perfect Paperback, 2011.

Exploring The Difference It Makes

www.ingramcontent.com/pod-product-compliance
Lightning Source LLC
Chambersburg PA
CBHW062111290426
44110CB00023B/2783